W9-AXM-592

hide
this
french
book 101

Berlitz Publishing
New York   Munich   Singapore

Hide This French Book 101

NO part of this book may be reproduced, stored in a retrieval system or transmitted in any form or means electronic, mechanical, photocopying, recording or otherwise, without prior written permission from Apa Publications.

Contacting the Editors
Every effort has been made to provide accurate information in this publication, but changes are inevitable. The publisher cannot be responsible for any resulting loss, inconvenience or injury. We would appreciate it if readers would call our attention to any errors or outdated information by contacting Berlitz Publishing, 193 Morris Avenue, Springfield, NJ 07081, USA. email: comments@berlitzbooks.com

All Rights Reserved
© 2006 Berlitz Publishing/APA Publications GmbH & Co. Verlag KG, Singapore Branch, Singapore

Berlitz Trademark Reg. U.S. Patent Office and other countries. Marca Registrada. Used under license from Berlitz Investment Corporation.

First Printing: Spring 2006
Printed in China

ISBN 981-246-760-2

Writer: Eve-Alice Roustang Stoller
Editorial Director: Sheryl Olinsky Borg
Senior Editor/Project Manager: Lorraine Sova
Assistant Editor: Emily Bernath
Production Manager: Elizabeth Gaynor
Cover and Interior Design: Blair Swick, Wee Design Group
Illustrations: Kyle Webster, Amy Zaleski

101

best French expressions

table of contents

*Hide This French Book **101*** is the ultimate collection of French phrases and expressions. It's a countdown of the coolest language—from what's trendy to what's taboo. In addition to the **101** very best expressions, check out the ᵗʰᵉ**A**-ₗᵢₛₜ, which highlights the lingo you've gotta know. But don't stop there—look for 🌡 and 🌡 , which tip you off to the hottest—that is, most vulgar—language. Add 'em all together and you get a ton of very cool French.

intro

Warning: This language can get you into trouble. If you wanna say it in public, that's up to you. But we're not taking the rap (like responsibility and liability) for any problems you could encounter by using the expressions in *Hide This French Book 101*. These include, but are not limited to, verbal and/or physical abuse, bar brawls, cat fights, arrest…. Use caution when dealing with French that's hot!

Salut!

sah-lew

Hi!

It's short and sweet.

2

Hé!
eh

Yo!

Get someone's attention.

the basics

Ça va?
sah vah

How are you?

It's the quick way to say "Comment ça va?"

the basics

4

Quoi de neuf?

kwah duh nuhf

What's up?

Literally: What's new?

the basics

5

Ça boume?
sah boom

How's it going?

Literally: Is it blasting?

the basics

6

Ça gaze?
sah gahz

Doing well?

Literally: Is it gazing?

7

Vous là-bas!
voo lah-bah

You!

This can be considered rude if said to someone you don't know.

the basics

Ouh, ouh!

oo oo

Yoo-hoo!

A wild call for attention...

the basics

9

Tu me gonfles!

tew muh gohN-fluh

You're getting on my nerves!

Literally: You make me swell!

the basics

Fils de pute!

fees duh pewt

Son of a bitch!

You've got to be really pissed off to use this insult.

the basics

the A-list

the best ways to say "cool"

Cool! kooool
Cool!
Say it with a "cool" French accent, of course.

Sympa! saN-pah
Nice!

Extra! ex-trah
Super!

Tip-top! teep-tawp
Very cool!

Pile-poil! peel-pwahl
Perfect!

D'enfer! dahN-fair
Great!

Literally: From hell!

Géant! zhay-ahN
Great!

Génial! zhay-nyahl
Sweet! / Brilliant!

Literally: Genius!

C'est de la mort qui tue!
seh duh lah mawr kee tew
Killer!

Literally: It's deadly killing!

Depending on the context, this phrase can mean it's killer in a good way or a bad way.

11

À tout.
ah toot

See you soon.

*This is a quick, cute way to say
"à tout à l'heure", literally,
within the hour.*

the basics

Ciao! / Tchao!

chow

Bye!

*The Italian "ciao" is so popular,
the French have taken it over
and provided an alternate, French
spelling of the word.*

the basics

13

Tu es trop sexy.
tew eh troh sex-ee

You're really sexy.

Thanks for the compliment.

14

Vous êtes mannequin?
voo zet mahn-neh-kaN

Are you a model?

A little flattery can go a long way.

romance

Puis-je t'offrir quelque chose à boire?

pwee-zhuh toff-reer kel-kuh shohz ah bwahr

Can I get you a drink?

Who would say no?!

romance

Ça vous dérange si je m'asseois ici?

sah voo day-rahNzh see zhuh mah-swah ee-see

Do you mind if I sit here?

Get a little closer.

romance

17

Casse-toi!
kahss twah

Go away!

Aren't interested, huh?!

romance

18

Laissez-moi tranquille, s'il vous plaît.

les-say mwah trahN-keel seel voo pleh

Leave me alone, please.

It's polite yet firm.

romance

19

Va voir ailleurs si j'y suis!

vah vwah ah-yur see zhee swee

Get the heck out of here!

Literally: Go somewhere else—see if I'm there!

*Rest assured, that guy or girl won't
bother you again if you use this rejection.*

romance

20

Tu t'es pas regardé(e)!
tew teh pah ruh-gah-day

Take a good look at yourself!

Literally: You haven't seen yourself!

romance

21

Cette fille, je la kiffe.

set fee-yuh zhuh lah kiff

I like that girl.

"Kiffe" is from the Arabic verb for "love".

romance

22

Ce mec me branche.
suh mek muh brahNsh

I like that guy.

Literally: That guy plugs me in.

romance

23

Tu es SBAB!
tew eh ess-bay-ah-bay

You're super good to @#&!

It stands for "Super Bonne À Baiser".

romance

Tu as fait un test HIV?

tew ah feh aN test ahsh-ee-veh

Have you been tested for HIV?

Ask the right questions...

romance

25

Tu prends la pilule?

tew prahN lah pee-lewl

Are you on the pill?

romance

Non. Mets une capote.

nohN meh ewn kah-pawt

No. Put on a condom.

romance

27

Es-tu gay?
eh-tew gay

Are you gay?

What a loaded question...

romance

Sors du placard!

sawr dew plah-kahr

Come out of the closet!

You've got really good gaydar, huh?!

romance

the A-list

the best pet names

mon amour mohN ah-moor
my love

mon bébé mohN beh-beh
my baby

mon cœur mohN kuhr
my darling
Literally: my heart

mon chou mohN shoo
my dear
Literally: my cabbage

ma biche ♀ mah beesh
my doe

mon lapin mohN lah-paN
my sweetie
Literally: my rabbit

mon trésor mohN tray-zawr
my treasure

29

J'ai flirté avec lui.
zhay fler-tay ah-vek lwee

I made out with him.

Good for you!

romance

30

On s'est mis à poil.

ohN seh mee ah pwahl

We got naked.

Literally: We wore only our body hair.

romance

31

Il/Elle m'a allumé(e).

eel/el mah ah-lew-may

He/She led me on.

Literally: He/She lit me.

Though you can use "allumer" for both sexes, it's usually applied to women. "Une allumeuse" is a tease—for her only!

romance

32

C'est fini entre nous.
seh fee-nee ahN-truh noo

It's over between us.

Be firm!

romance

33

Tu es tellement branché(e)!

tew eh tel-mahN brahN-shay

You're so trendy!

"Branché" literally means "plugged in".

lookin' good

34

Ce style est complètement niais.

suh steel eh kohN-plet-mahN nee-ay

This style is completely cheesy.

Call the fashion police...

lookin' good

On va faire des courses?

ohN vah fair day koors

Are we going shopping?

Get that cool Parisian look.

lookin' good

C'est un beau morceau.

set aN bo maw-so

He/She is a handsome morsel.

Absolutely delicious, right?!

lookin' good

Miam miam!
mee-yahm mee-yahm

Mmmm!

Make this gesture as
someone tasty walks by.

38

Quel canon!
kel kah-nohN

What a knock-out!

It's usually said with the mouth wide open.

lookin' good

39

C'est un boudin.

set aN boo-daN

She is an ugly woman.

Literally: She is blood sausage.

lookin' good

40

Il est maigre comme un clou.
eel eh meh-gruh kom aN kloo

He is skin and bones.

Literally: He is skinny as a nail.

lookin' good

Il/Elle s'est fait tatouer.

eel/el seh feh tah-too-ay

He/She got a tattoo.

A permanent memory of your trip to France...

lookin' good

42

Il/Elle a un piercing au nombril.

eel/el ah aN peer-sing oh nohN-breel

He/She has a belly button piercing.

Must've hurt.

lookin' good

43

Tu as fait de la chirurgie esthétique?

tew ah feh duh lah sheer-ewr-zhee es-tay-teek

Did you have plastic surgery?

Can you tell?

lookin' good

44

Je me suis fait refaire le nez.

zhuh muh swee feh ruh-fair luh nay

I had a nose job.

Gotta put your best face forward, right?!

lookin' good

45

Je me suis fait gonfler les lèvres.

zhuh muh swee feh gohN-flay lay lehv-ruh

I had my lips enhanced.

Pucker up!

lookin' good

46

J'ai besoin de pisser.
zhay buh-swahN duh pee-say

I have to piss.

Thanks for the announcement.

lookin' good

47

Quel désastre! J'ai la diarrhée.

kel day-zahs-truh zhay lah dyah-ray

What a disaster! I have diarrhea.

Sucks to be you.

lookin' good

48

Tu pues la transpiration!

tew pew lah trahN-spee-rah-see-ohN

You've got BO!

Literally: You reek of perspiration!

lookin' good

Tu schlingues!
tew shlaNg

You stink!

Take a shower already...

lookin' good

50

T'es une ordure.

teh ewn aw-dewr

You're a scumbag.

"T'es" is the quick and easy way to say, "tu es", you are.

lookin' good

the A-list

the best ways to insult someone

T'es... teh
You're…

un minable ♂ aN mee-nah-bluh
a pathetic guy

un pauvre type ♂ aN poh-vruh teep
a loser

une pouffiasse ♀ ! ewn poof-fyahss
a slut

une salope ♀ ! ewn sah-lawp
a bitch

On va faire la fête!

ohN vah fair lah fett

Let's party!

What are you in the mood for?

havin' fun

52

On va en boîte.

ohN vah ahN bwaht

Let's go clubbing.

Have a good time clubbing in Paris.

havin' fun

53

Quel clubeur, celui-là!
kel _kluh-buhr suh-lwee lah

He's really club crazy!

Oh, really?!

havin' fun

54

Je fais une petite soirée.

zhuh feh ewn puh-teet swah-ray

I'm having a small get-together.

Party at your house!

havin' fun

Est-ce qu'il y a une discothèque en ville?

ess keel yah ewn dees-koh-tek ahN veel

Is there a dance club in town?

If you're in any major French city, there is bound to be at least one!

havin' fun

the A-list

trendy French drinks

pastis pahs-teess
anise-flavored alcohol, usually mixed
with water

shuters carambar
shew-tair kah-rahm-bah
caramel-flavored candy dissolved in vodka

fraise tagada frez tah-gah-dah
strawberry-flavored gummy candy
dissolved in vodka

vodka orange   vohd-kah oh-rahNzh
screwdriver

blanc-cassis   blahN kah-seess
white wine + black currant syrup

panaché   pah-nah-shay
beer + lemonade

monaco   moh-nah-koh
beer + grenadine

56

Je t'offre une bière?
zhuh tawf-fruh ewn bee-yair

Can I buy you a beer?

Try a Belgian beer; you'll be happy you did.

havin' fun

Tu veux un verre?
tew vuh aN vair

Do you want a shot?

The fast way to get a party started...

havin' fun

Ça s'arrose!

sah sah-rawz

Let's celebrate!

Literally: Let's sprinkle!

It's cute and classy.

havin' fun

Tchin, tchin!
cheen cheen

Cheers!

Raise your glass when you make this toast.

havin' fun

Je suis pompette!

zhuh swee pum-pet

I'm tipsy!

Too much champagne?!

havin' fun

havin' fun

Complètement bourré(e)!

kohN-plet-mahN boo-ray

Completely drunk!

This gesture is the best way to
announce that someone is
totally smashed.

havin' fun

62

Tu fumes?
tew fewm

Do you smoke?

Lighting up is still a popular pastime for many...

havin' fun

On s'en grille une?

ohN sahN gree ewn

Want to have a smoke?

Literally: Do you want to grate one?

havin' fun

the A-list

the best ways to say "cigarette"

une clope ewn klawp

une garo ewn gah-roh

une nuigrav ewn nwee-grahv

It's from, "nuit gravement à la santé," very dangerous for your health, the warning label on a pack of cigarettes.

the scoop

There isn't a minimum age to buy cigarettes in France. You'll find few smoke-free areas—smoking restrictions apply mainly to healthcare facilities, schools, offices, buses, and taxis—and smoking is allowed and accepted almost everywhere. Walk into just about any restaurant or bar in France, and the air is smoke-filled. Law requires restaurants and bars to have a smoking and a non-smoking section, but it's rarely enforced.

havin' fun

64

Jouons!
zhoo-ohN

Let's play!

Get active already!

havin' fun

Allez!

ah-lay

Go!

C'mon—more it!

havin' fun

66

Tous ensemble!
toos ahN-sahN-bluh

All together!

Push your team to keep goin'!

havin' fun

67

Bouffez-les! / Explosez-les!
boof-ay lay   ex-ploh-say-lay

Get them!

Literally: Eat them! / Explode them!

havin' fun

68

Va te coucher!

vah tuh koo-shay

You suck!

Literally: Go to bed!

havin' fun

Quel nul!

kel newl

He sucks!

Literally: What a zero!

havin' fun

70

Retourne au vestiaire!

ruh-toorn oh ves-tyair

Kick him out!

Literally: Go to the locker room!

havin' fun

Vendu, l'arbitre!

vahN-dew lah-bee-truh

The referee took a bribe!

Literally: Paid for!

havin' fun

72

Quel merde, ce joueur!
kel maird suh zhoo-uhr

@#&! this player!

Sometimes you've gotta swear.

havin' fun

73

Immanquable!
aN-mahN-kah-bluh

How could you miss that?!

Literally: Can't be missed!

havin' fun

Téléphoné!

tay-lay-fun-ay

So predictable!

Literally: Telephoned!

havin' fun

75

Dégueulasse!

day-guh-lahss

Foul!

.

What a game!

havin' fun

76

J'en ai plein le cul.
zhahN nay plaN luh kew

I'm sick of it.

Literally: I have my ass full.

havin' fun

J'en peux plus.
zhahN puh plew

I can't take it anymore.

That was some workout, huh?!

havin' fun

78

J'ai la pêche.

zhay lah pesh

I feel great.

Literally: I have the peach.

havin' fun

Je suis en forme.

zhuh swee zahN fawrm

I'm in shape.

All that exercise has paid off!

havin' fun

80

Je veux faire du saut en parachute.

zhuh vuh fair dew soht ahN pah-rah-shewt

I want to go skydiving.

Think you've got the guts?

havin' fun

Tu veux faire du saut à l'élastique?

tew vuh fair dew soht ah lay-lahss-teek

Want to go bungee jumping?

Adrenaline junkie!

havin' fun

82

Tu veux jouer aux cartes?
tew vuh zhoo-ay oh kahrt

Do you want to play cards?

*Gambling can be an entertaining—
if not expensive—pastime.*

havin' fun

Est-ce qu'il y a un casino en ville?

ess keel yah aN kah-zee-noh ahN veel

Is there a casino in town?

Ever heard of Monte Carlo?!

havin' fun

84

Où est l'hippodrome?
oo eh leep-oh-drawm

Where's the racetrack?

Got a good tip on a winner?

havin' fun

On se fait une belote?

ohN suh feh ewn bel-awt

Wanna play belote?

"La belote" has been the unofficial national game of France for almost a century and is so popular, it's even featured in some French gangster films.

havin' fun

86

Tu veux risquer le paquet?

tew vuh rees-kay luh pah-keh

Do you want to put all your money down?

Got euros to burn?

havin' fun

87

J'ai la main.

zhay lah maN

I have the deal.

Literally: I have the hand.

havin' fun

88

Je me couche.
zhuh muh koosh

I fold.

Literally: I'm going to sleep.

havin' fun

Tu as perdu au jeu?

tew ah pair-dew oh zhuh

Did you gamble it away?

Hope you've got a ride home...

havin' fun

the scoop

The first French casino was opened in 1863 in Monte Carlo, on the French Riviera. Monte Carlo is still a hotspot for upscale gamblers—only the trendiest table games are on offer: American and European roulette; blackjack; poker; "chemin de fer", a game similar to baccarat; and more. If table games aren't your thing, there are more than 1000 slot machines and tons of video poker terminals where you can test your luck. You've gotta be 18 or older to play and must wear "suitable attire" to enter (i.e., don't show up in your bikini and cut-off shorts). If you wanna play with the big guns, you'll have to wear a suit and tie (gentlemen) or evening dress (ladies) after 11 pm in private playing rooms.

Quelle est ton adresse e-mail?

kel eh tohN ah-dress ee-mail

What's your e-mail address?

"Courriel" and "mél" are also used for e-mail, though much less frequently.

tech talk

91

Tu as vu ce super ordi.
tew ah vew suh sew-pair aw-dee

Check out this cool computer.

*"Ordi" is the quick way to say
"ordinateur", computer.*

tech talk

92

Mon ordi a planté.
mohN naw-dee ah plahN-tay

My computer crashed.

Hope you're good at troubleshooting.

tech talk

93

Où est le point d'accès Wifi le plus proche?

oo eh luh pwahN dahk-seh wee fee luh plew prawsh

Where is the closest hotspot?

Hotspot here means Wi-Fi® area, not a trendy locale.

tech talk

Quel est ton chatroom préféré?

kel eh tohN chaht-room pray-fair-ay

What's your favorite chatroom?

Romance, fashion, sports, news—the list of chatrooms is endless!

tech talk

95

slt (Salut.)

Hi.

*Start your chat with a simple,
short greeting.*

tech talk

ASV (âge, sexe, ville)

A/S/L (age, sex, location)

Before things go too far,
ask about 'em...

tech talk

97

biz (Bisous.)
X (Kiss.)

Love on-line...

tech talk

98

MDR (mort de rire)
LOL (laugh out loud)

Literally: dead from laughing

What's so funny?!

tech talk

the **A**-list

<u>tech words you've gotta know</u>

recherche ruh-shairsh
search

aide ed
help

supprimer sew-pree-may
delete

répondre ray-pohN-druh
reply

répondre à tous ray-pohN-druh ah toos
reply all

transférer trahNs-fair-ray
forward

bloquer blaw-kay
block

sauvegarder sohv-gah-day
save

imprimer aN-pree-may
print

sortir saw-teer
log out

99

Appelle-moi.
ah-pell-mwah

Call me.

Maybe you'd rather send a text message?

tech talk

100

koi29? (Quoi de neuf?)

What's up?

Keep your "textos", text messages, brief!

tech talk

101

@+ (À plus tard.)

CUL8R (See you later.)

tech talk